This book belongs to

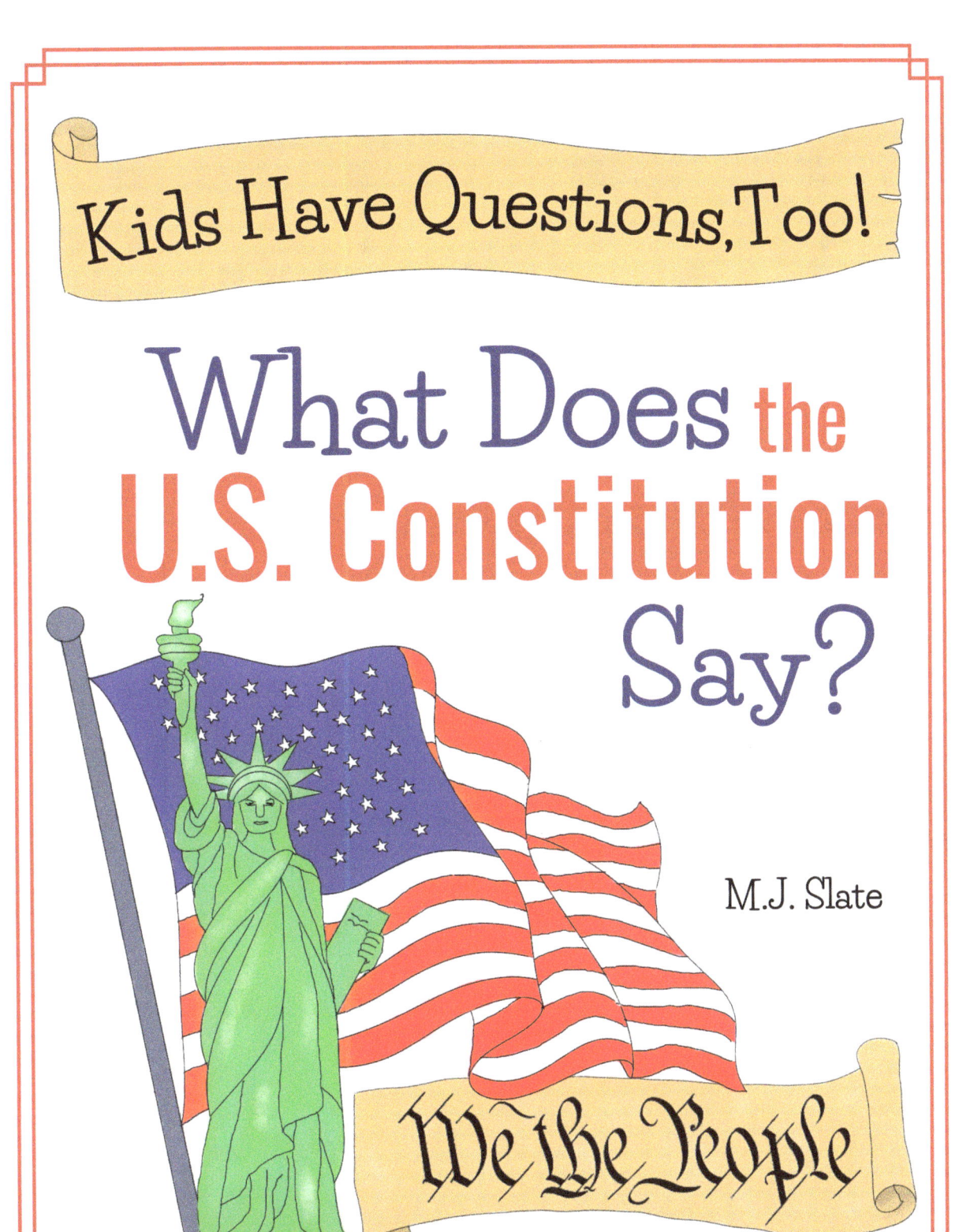

Kids Have Questions, Too!

What Does the U.S. Constitution Say?

M.J. Slate

We the People

To my kids with all of their endless questions.
I hope this answers some of them for you.

Kids Have Questions, Too!
What Does the U.S. Constitution Say?

Copyright © 2021 by M.J. Slate

All rights reserved. No part of this book may be reproduced in any form, or by any means, without prior written permission from the publisher.

ISBN (hardcover) 978-1-7335322-2-8
ISBN (paperback) 978-1-7335322-3-5
ISBN (ebook) 978-1-7335322-4-2

Requests for permissions should be sent to:
contact@QuillandTome.com

Quill and Tome Publishing
www.quillandtome.com

In the 1700s, Great Britain controlled the thirteen American colonies.

The 13 Colonies

Great Britain

The colonists were unhappy.

They felt they were not being treated fairly and did not have enough say in the way they were governed.

The colonists demanded rights, fairer taxes, and more representation in the government.

When this didn't happen, the colonists began to rebel.

After being denied over and over again, the colonists had enough.

The rebellion became a war for independence.

In July of 1776, fifty-six men from the thirteen colonies signed the Declaration of Independence.

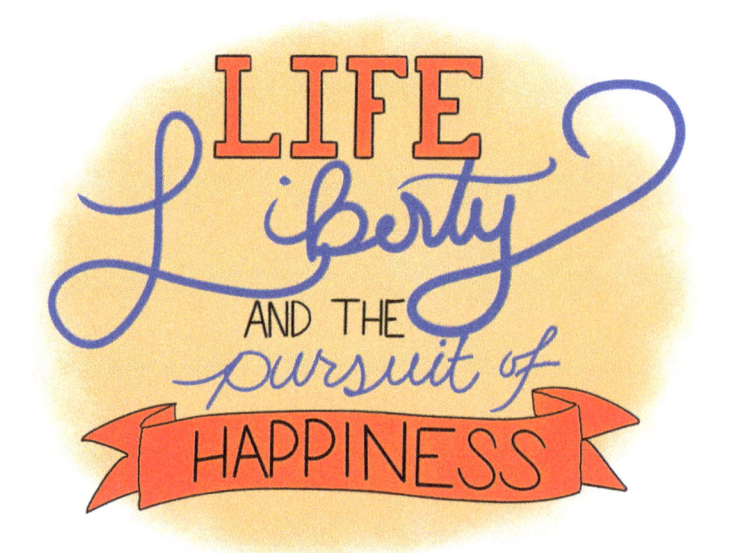

LIFE
Liberty
AND THE
pursuit of
HAPPINESS

Finally, a free and independent nation was born.

After the colonists won their
independence, the colonies
became states.

Each state went about its own
business, and each state had
its own laws and money.

But something was not right.

The states were not working well
together. They were too divided.

The colonists knew if they were
to succeed as a united country,
they had to come up with a solution.

In 1781, all thirteen states signed the Articles of Confederation.

The Articles of Confederation unified the states under the United States of America.

It protected individual freedoms, defended states' rights, and created a national currency.

UNITED UNDER
A League of Friendship

INDIVIDUAL FREEDOMS

NATIONAL CURRENCY
0

STATES' RIGHTS

Rhode Island   Pennsylvania   New Jersey
Connecticut   New Hampshire   Massachusetts
Virginia   New York   Maryland   Georgia
North Carolina   Delaware   South Carolina

Yet, the Articles of Confederation
were not strong enough.

The federal government had certain
powers, but it could not make the
states obey them.

The states wanted to stay independent.
They wanted to keep the power
to make their own decisions.

Still, by 1787, the people could no
longer ignore the need for a stronger
central government to help the
states work together.

Each state sent representatives
to a meeting to fix the
Articles of Confederation.

The men who showed up to this meeting are now known as the Founding Fathers.

They agreed on many reasons to write the Constitution.

They wanted the states to work together.

They wanted the country to be able to defend itself.

Most of all, they wanted to secure liberty for themselves and all Americans who came after them.

Thomas Jefferson   John Adams   George Washington   Benjamin Franklin   James Madison

Still, they disagreed on how the country should be set up to reach those goals.

Some wanted the president elected for life.

Others said that was too much like a king.

Some said the small states should have as much say as the bigger states.

Others said the larger states should have the most say.

The debate lasted all summer as they
tried to consider all the states' wishes.

The Founding Fathers eventually
came to an agreement called
"The Great Compromise".

They knew the United States
could not grow without change.

So, the Founding Fathers wrote the
Constitution with the future in mind.

They made it a living document,
meaning it could be changed over time.

The Constitution is the
supreme law of the land.

It lays out the responsibilities of the
government and the rights of the people.

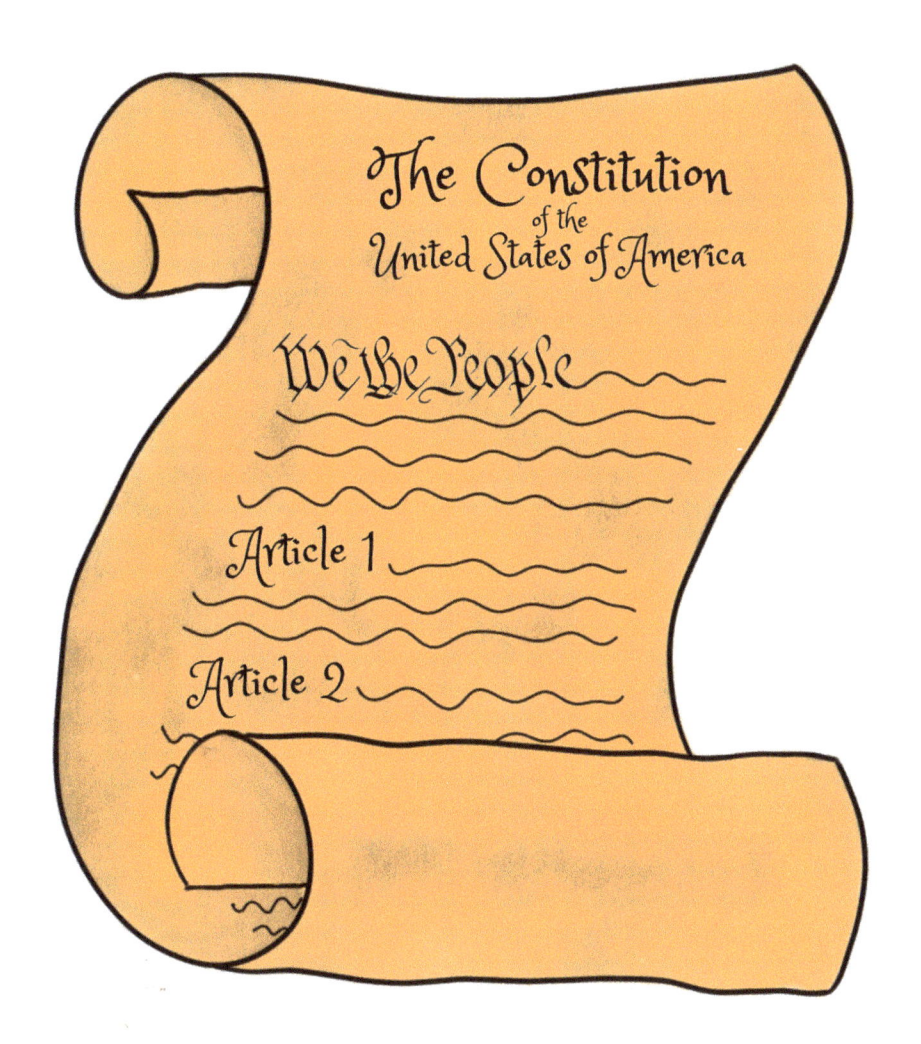

The first part of the Constitution
is called the Preamble.

It tells why the Founding Fathers wrote
the Constitution in the first place.

It states the basic principles for
keeping the American people free.

WE the PEOPLE
of the United States

The Preamble

"We the People of the United States,
in Order to form a more perfect Union,
establish Justice,
insure domestic Tranquility,
provide for the common defence,
promote the general Welfare,
and secure the Blessings of Liberty
to ourselves and our Posterity,
do ordain and establish
this Constitution
for the United States of America."

Article 1

Article 1 of the Constitution lays out the powers of the Legislative Branch.

The Legislature is also known as Congress.

Congress is the law-making part of the government. They can write laws, charge taxes, print money, and even declare war.

The Founding Fathers compromised on
how much power the states should have.

They created two houses in the Legislature:
The Senate and
The House of Representatives.

The Senate would have two senators
from each state regardless of size.

The House of Representatives
would have members based on the
size of that state's population.

Both houses have to
approve every law.

Article 2

Article 2 of the Constitution lays out the powers of the Executive Branch.
The President and their Cabinet make up this part of the government.

The President acts as Commander-in-Chief of the Armed Forces.

14

It is the President's job to appoint members of the Cabinet and Justices to the Supreme Court.

The President must sign the laws before they can take effect.

It is also the President's job to see that the laws are executed and enforced.

The President holds office for a four-year term and can serve a total of two terms.

Article 3

Article 3 of the Constitution lays out the powers of the Judicial Branch.

The Judicial Branch is made up of the Supreme Court and lower federal courts.

The Supreme Court can handle all cases that have to do with the Constitution and the laws of the United States.

The Supreme Court is the highest in the land.

It consists of nine judges, known as justices.

The justices are appointed by the President and approved by Congress.

Congress can also establish lower courts to serve under the Supreme Court.

17

Article 4

Article 4 discusses the relationship between the states and the federal government.

This section of the Constitution sets up the way the states can work together and side by side.

Each state is unique and can have its own laws.

Citizens can enjoy the freedoms of other states, but they must also obey the laws of other states.

This section of the Constitution also states the federal government will protect and defend the states against invasion and violence.

Article 5

Article 5 lays out the process we must follow to amend the Constitution.

The Founding Fathers knew that, over time, there would be changes they could not foresee.

Change CAN BE A GOOD THING

Amendments allow us to update the Constitution instead of replacing it.

Congress

First, ⅔ of Congress must think an amendment is necessary before anything can happen.

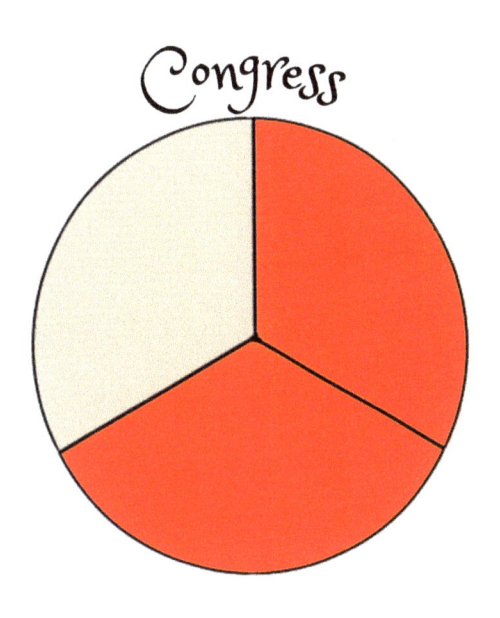

The States

Then, ¾ of all states must ratify, or approve, the amendment before it can become law.

21

Article 6

Article 6 establishes
the Constitution as the
supreme law of the land.

Even though states can have their
own laws, all states must support
the Constitution.

This section says that nobody
should have to take a religious test
to hold a government position.

United States Constitution

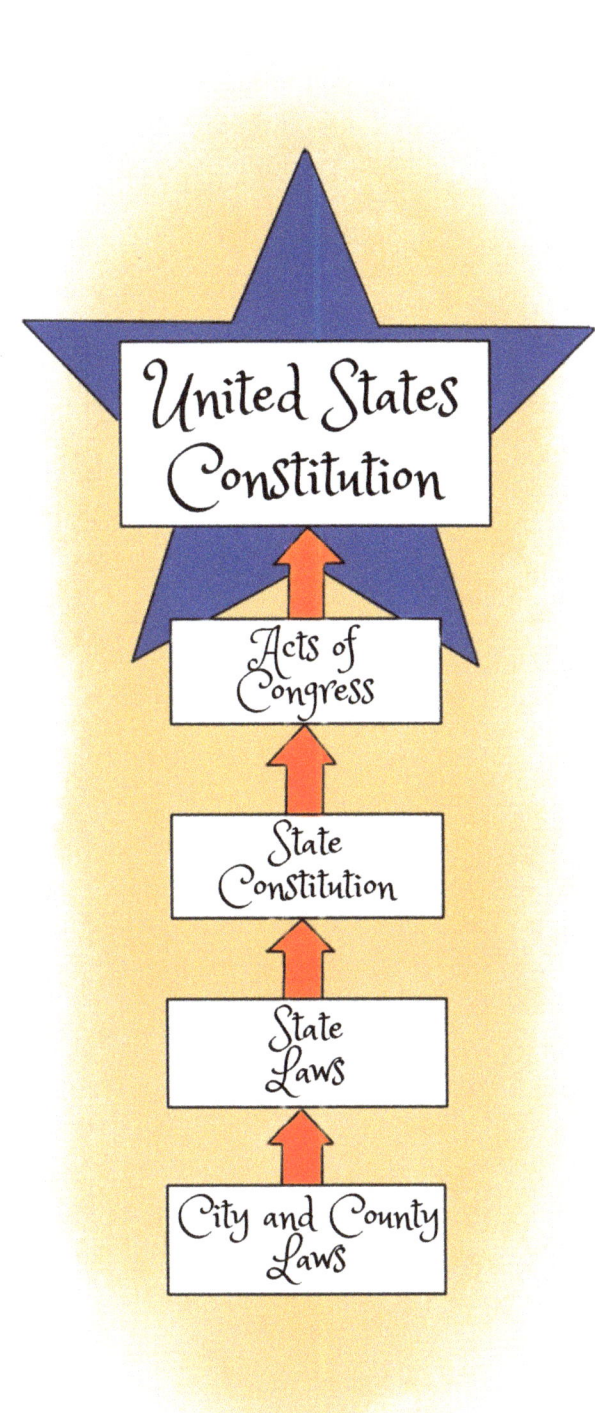

Acts of Congress

State Constitution

State Laws

City and County Laws

It also holds the United States accountable for repaying any money it borrows.

23

Article 7

Article 7 set up the process the Constitution needed to follow to take effect for the first time.

It required nine out of the thirteen original states to ratify the Constitution.

Delaware became the first state to ratify the Constitution on December 7, 1787.

The other states soon followed.

When New Hampshire became the ninth state to ratify on June 21, 1788, the Constitution became law.

In 1789, George Washington was elected the first president of the United States.

All thirteen states ratified the Constitution by the middle of 1790.

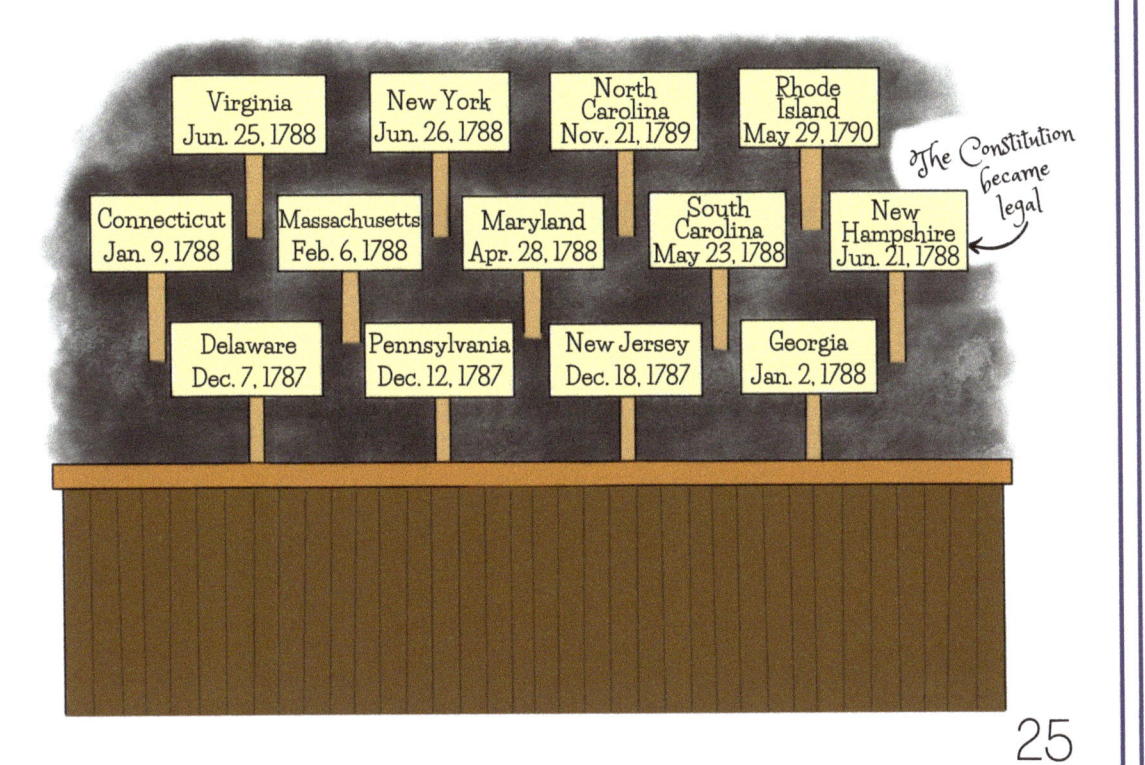

Virginia Jun. 25, 1788	New York Jun. 26, 1788	North Carolina Nov. 21, 1789	Rhode Island May 29, 1790
Connecticut Jan. 9, 1788	Massachusetts Feb. 6, 1788	Maryland Apr. 28, 1788	South Carolina May 23, 1788	New Hampshire Jun. 21, 1788
Delaware Dec. 7, 1787	Pennsylvania Dec. 12, 1787	New Jersey Dec. 18, 1787	Georgia Jan. 2, 1788

The Constitution became legal ← (New Hampshire Jun. 21, 1788)

The Bill of Rights

The Founding Fathers wrote the Constitution to list the government's rights and responsibilities.

In 1791, the First Congress passed the Bill of Rights as a way to further protect individual liberties.

| 1st FREEDOM of EXPRESSION | 2nd RIGHT to BEAR ARMS | 3rd QUARTERING of SOLDIERS | 4th unreasonable SEARCH & SEIZURE | 5th due PROCESS of LAW |

It states the American people have freedom of speech and religion, and the right to bear arms.

It guarantees the privacy and rights of those accused of crimes.

Freedoms OF THE PEOPLE

The Bill of Rights also states the powers not given to the federal government are given to the people and the state governments.

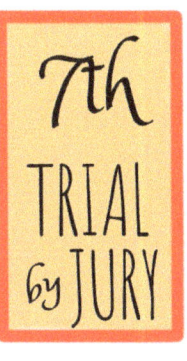

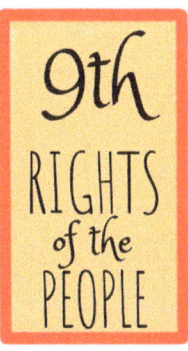

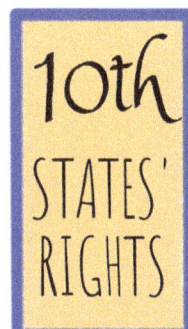

6th RIGHT to a FAIR TRIAL

7th TRIAL by JURY

8th CRUEL & UNUSUAL punishment

9th RIGHTS of the PEOPLE

10th STATES' RIGHTS

The 3 Branches of Government

Executive Branch

Enforces laws
4-year term

President

Vice President

The Cabinet:
Agriculture
Commerce
Defense
Education
Energy
Health and Human Services
Homeland Security
Housing and Urban Development
Interior
Labor
State
Transportation
Treasury
Veterans Affairs
Justice

Legislative Branch
Makes laws
Also called Congress

House of Representatives
435 members
Elected from states
based on population
2-year term

Senate
100 members
2 elected from each state
6-year term

Judicial Branch
Explains and applies laws

Supreme Court
9 Justices
Appointed for life

Lower Courts

The men who wrote the Constitution in 1787 designed a completely new form of government.

They left out details that would limit and date the Constitution.

They provided only the basic framework, leaving room to amend it over time.

This new form of government has worked better than the Founding Fathers could have hoped.

In over 200 years, only a total of 27 amendments have been added to the Constitution.

The first 10 were the Bill of Rights that were added the very first year.

The way the Constitution can change over time is one of the things that makes the American form of government so unique.

The Constitution endures as a strong symbol of freedom, liberty, and independence.

Glossary

ratify - to approve or confirm

law - a rule set by the state or federal government

accountable - to be held responsible for an action

compromise - to settle an argument

representation - to show up on behalf of personal interest

colonies - communities under the political control of another country

posterity - future generations of people

liberty - freedom within laws of society

freedom - the power to act, think, or speak without restriction

independence - freedom from another's control

justice - fair behavior and treatment of all citizens

Printed in the USA
CPSIA information can be obtained
at www.ICGtesting.com
LVHW051603120824
788025LV00003B/28

9 781733 532228